Evaluating Investment Opportunities

Due Diligence

Student Edition

Books by the Authors

Fundamentals of Angel Investing
A Guide to the Principles, Skills and Concepts Every Angel Investor Needs to Succeed

Angel Investing by the Numbers
Valuation, Capitalization, Portfolio Construction and Startup Economics

Leaders Wanted: Making Startup Deals Happen
Advanced Techniques in Deal Leadership and Due Diligence for Early Stage Investors

Guide, Advise and Inspire: How Startup Boards Drive Growth and Exits
An Overview of the Principles, Skills and Concepts Every Early Stage Company Board Member Needs to Succeed

Venture Capital: A Practical Guide
A Guide to Fund Formation and Management

Angel Investing Course Books by the Authors

Angel 101 and Angel 201
Introduction to Angel Investing

Due Diligence
Evaluating Investment Opportunities

Termsheets and Valuations
Negotiating Investments

Portfolio Success and Startup Economics
Angel Finance

Evaluating Investment Opportunities

Due Diligence

Student Edition

Hambleton Lord
Christopher Mirabile

Seraf
Compass
Publications

www.seraf-investor.com

Copyright © 2018 by Seraf LLC

All rights reserved. No part of this publication may be reproduced, distributed, or transmitted in any form or by any means, including photocopying, recording, or other electronic or mechanical methods, without the prior written permission of the publisher, except in the case of brief quotations embodied in critical reviews and certain other noncommercial uses permitted by copyright law. For permission requests, contact the publisher, addressed "Attention: Permissions Coordinator," at the address below.

support@seraf-investor.com

www.seraf-investor.com

Cover Illustration Copyright: lublubachka / 123RF Stock Photo

Table of Contents

1. **Introduction - Evaluating Investment Opportunities**   1

2. **Short Course - Fundamentals of Due Diligence**   3
   - 2.1. Introduction   7
   - 2.2. 10 Key Risks in Early Stage Investing   10
   - 2.3. Investment Thesis / WNTBB / Lessons Learned   15
   - 2.4. Due Diligence Resources   17

3. **Long Course - Essentials of Due Diligence**   23
   - 3.1. Introduction   27
   - 3.2. Rule #1: It's All About the Team   31
   - 3.3. Product / Technology / Intellectual Property   35
   - 3.4. Market Opportunity / Go-to-Market Strategy / Competition   41
   - 3.5. Financials / Funding / Legal / Exits   51
   - 3.6. Investment Thesis / WNTBB / Lessons Learned   63
   - 3.7. Due Diligence Resources   65

Appendix

- I. Overview   71
- II. Due Diligence Report Template   73
- III. Due Diligence Checklist   83
- IV. Customer Reference Check Questionnaire   91
- V. Management Assessment Questionnaire   95

Introduction
Evaluating Investment Opportunities

Some investors will tell you after spending 60 minutes with an entrepreneur they know in their gut whether to make an investment. They rely on their instincts and sometimes their ability to "pattern match" with successful opportunities and entrepreneurs they worked with in their past.

At the other end of the spectrum, there are investors who will spend countless hours digging into every aspect of a startup company. They want to feel 100% confident in their investment decision before they sign the check. But this is a fallacy. Early stage companies are inherently risky because they are typically newly formed teams, using new technologies or methods, to crack into markets that are often new, if they exist at all. You cannot fully de-risk that kind of investment - at some point it is about weighing the huge upside potential against the probability of failure. Comprehensive due diligence efforts beyond a certain point aren't always helpful - they like this usually drag on for months and may do relatively little to actually de-risk the deal.

What is challenging to explain is that both types of investors meet with some success, and both types meet with some failure. Because so much judgment is involved in investing, it can be very hard to know what the right amount of diligence is, and how to go about it. It turns out that picking the right level of diligence is achievable: due diligence is really nothing more than the gathering of additional facts which you can consider before making a decision. If you need to make a decision, it will generally be easier if you have some data. There is no specific amount necessary, and not all data will be directly helpful with the decision. The amount will vary by stage of company. But good data, timely and efficiently gathered, will never hurt.

Our Approach to Due Diligence

Accordingly, in our roles as Managing Directors at Launchpad Venture Group, we believe in a balanced approach to due diligence. As my partner, Christopher likes to say: "We major on the majors." Put another way, we are not trying to predict the future in great detail, we are just trying to uncover key issues and avoid making really obvious mistakes. Diligence is nothing more than trying to find those 2-3 things which might otherwise have caused your future self to say "if I had known that at the time I would never have invested." Over the years and after making investments in over 100 companies, we designed a process that is intended to be quick, efficient and focused on the key issues which underpin the key risks. Executed properly our process can be completed in under 40 aggregate person hours of effort. Split this effort across a team of investors and you have a very fast and manageable project.

Before you take one of our courses on *"Evaluating Investment Opportunities"*, it's important to be reminded of and understand the stage of company we are typically examining. We invest very early in a company's lifespan. Usually, the company is pre-revenue, or in the early stages of revenue; up to a maximum of about $1M in annual revenue. So to be clear, we aren't talking about businesses with substantial operating histories, multiple divisions, multiple geographies, large teams or complex product portfolios. In the parlance of early stage investors, we are looking at companies during their Series Seed or Series A rounds of investment.

What's in this Book?

There are two main sections in this book. The first section includes the slides for a high level, 30 minute introductory class that we call the **"Fundamentals of Due Diligence"**. This class will introduce you to the three key steps of effective due diligence:
1. Identifying Key Risks
2. Developing the Investment Thesis
3. Acknowledging "What Needs to Be Believed" to Invest

The second section includes the slides for an in-depth, 2 hour class that we call the **"Essentials of Due Diligence"**. In addition to covering some of the materials discussed in the introductory class, we dig deep into helping you understand the types of questions we recommend you ask during diligence, major risks that should concern you, and how to structure deals to work well for founders and investors. The course will provide detailed material in four main areas:
1. Team
2. Product
3. Market
4. Financials

In addition to these two slide decks, we include an appendix with templates that help facilitate the due diligence process. In the appendix you will find:
1. Due Diligence Report Template
2. Due Diligence Checklist
3. Customer Reference Check Questionnaire
4. Management Assessment Questionnaire

By mastering the materials in this book, you should be confident that you can pull together a well executed due diligence effort that will ultimately lead to helping you increase the financial returns from your angel investments!

EVALUATING INVESTMENT OPPORTUNITIES
Fundamentals of Due Diligence

Angel Capital Association
World's Largest Association of Active Accredited Investors

ABOUT US

Vision

ACA is recognized as the trusted authority in angel investing.

- 13,000+ Investors
- 250+ Organizations
- Every US State and 5 Canadian Provinces
- Individual Angels, Angel Groups, Accredited Platforms, Family Offices

---

1 EVENTS
Host many international, national and regional events a year

2 EDUCATION
Provide gold standard education for angels

3 PUBLIC POLICY
Leading voice for angels on public policy lobbying in Washington, DC

4 DATA & RESEARCH
Central resource for angel investing data and research

Our Mission

Fuel the success of the accredited investor community through advocacy, education and connection building.

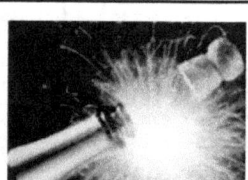

Welcome Message

Seraf's Philosophy

We believe investors in early stage companies should have access to best practices and professional tools to support the entrepreneurial community worldwide and achieve superior outcomes.

Insights and education, combined with powerful portfolio management tools allow investors to understand their investing better, learn faster and make necessary adjustments to select the highest quality opportunities and drive superior returns.

About the Authors

Ham is Co-Founder of Seraf and the Chairman of Launchpad Venture Group, a Boston-based angel group. Through his involvement with Launchpad, Ham has built a personal portfolio of 50+ early stage investments. In addition, he is a board member or board observer with 5 early stage companies.

Christopher is Chair Emeritus of the Angel Capital Association and Managing Director of Launchpad Venture Group. He helps manage Launchpad's portfolio of 70+ companies, he has personally invested in over 65 start-up companies, and is a limited partner in four specialized angel funds. Christopher is a board member, advisor and mentor to numerous start-ups, and a frequent panelist and speaker on entrepreneurship and angel-related topics.

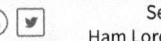
Seraf Co-Founders
Ham Lord & Christopher Mirabile

Presentation Overview

1   **ROLE OF DILIGENCE**
Avoiding Obvious Mistakes

2   **IDENTIFY KEY RISKS**
Without risk there is no reward

3   **DEVELOP INVESTMENT THESIS**
Establish Potential, Probability and Period

4   **ACKNOWLEDGE WNTBB**
What Needs to Be Believed

5   **LEARNING THE HARD WAY**
A few lessons learned

6   **APPENDIX**
Templates, Checklists and Questionnaires

Why Due Diligence is Important

Diligence is not about removing all risk and eliminating all mistakes

Investing at an early stage - lots of unknowns, there will be failures

Diligence is about spotting and avoiding the ***obvious*** mistakes

It's easy to imagine why things might work. It takes effort to grasp subtle and complex ways things can go wrong.

During Due Diligence, You Will...

Spend time with the management team

Educate yourself on the market

Understand the psyche of the target customer

Ask common sense questions

There is no right amount of diligence. Any diligence you do is better than none at all.

3 Guiding Principles of Due Diligence

Identify Key Risks

Develop the Investment Thesis

Acknowledge "What Needs to Be Believed" to Invest

Diligence is not about eliminating all risks and avoiding all mistakes. It's about spotting and avoiding the obvious ones.

Main Areas of Focus in Due Diligence

Team: Are they an "A" team or a "B" team?

Product: Are they selling a "Need to Have" or a "Nice to Have"?

Market: Is the market big enough?

No plan survives contact with the enemy. A great team can assess, learn and adapt quickly to survive and thrive. A good CEO pivots... a great CEO pivots in a capital efficient way.

Why Do We Do It?

A well executed diligence effort increases angel investment returns

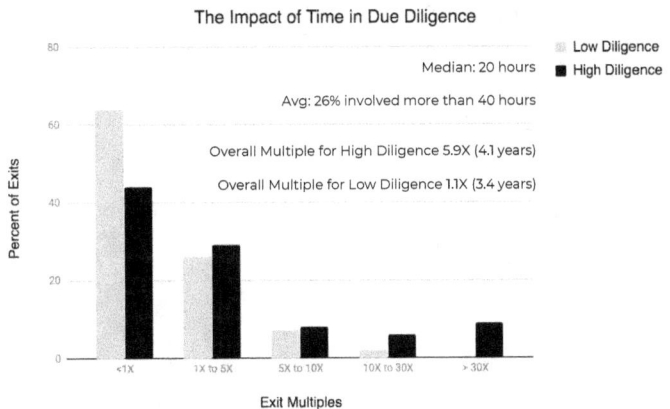

The Impact of Time in Due Diligence

Median: 20 hours
Avg: 26% involved more than 40 hours
Overall Multiple for High Diligence 5.9X (4.1 years)
Overall Multiple for Low Diligence 1.1X (3.4 years)

Mistakes are unavoidable, but racking up easily avoidable mistakes will hurt your overall returns.

10 Key Risks in Early Stage Investing

Risk is an inherent part, and necessary ingredient in all successful companies

The question is whether you understand the risks the company is taking, and have strategies to mitigate them

Without risk there can be no reward.

Team Risk

Conduct a thorough leadership assessment

- Review resumes
- Perform provided and "blind" reference checks
- Spend one-on-one time with the CEO

Look for people with integrity, tenacity, book learning and street smarts

I'd rather invest in an A team with a B plan, than a B team with an A plan.

Technical Risk

Does the widget exist yet? If not, is there a chance that it may be impossible to build?

Customer benefits matter. Benefits should approach a 10x improvement for the typical user.

A company that can hold their own in a detailed product roadmap review has a lot less technical risk than one that can't.

Market Adoption Risk

Ask customers and prospects the following...
- What problem does this product solve for you?
- Where does solving this problem fall on your priority list?
- Is your company generally an early adopter or late adopter?

Look for genuine demand or "pull" from a large enough segment of customers

If you build it, will they come?

Future Financing Risk

Know the macro market for financing

Know the benchmarks applied by those providing future capital

Look beyond the current round of financing, and ask the following:

- How much additional financing will the company need?
- Where will that money come from?
- Will it be available on reasonable terms?
- Who are the right investors for the company going forward?

Build a reasonable plan with the current financing round that allows some room for error.

Regulatory Risk

Are there any necessary permissions (e.g. FDA approval) to operate this business?

Not all regulatory situations introduce risk - sometimes they provide tailwinds; new rules may hasten adoption of a company's solution.

Regulatory approvals take time and money. Understand what is involved and watch for possible changes in the regulatory environment.

Competitive Risk

Understand the company's relative attractiveness alongside their competitors, and carve out a space with some enduring value

Competitors help educate the market, but they also

- Drive up the length of the sales cycle
- Undermine pricing power and compress margins
- Drive additional spend on R&D

Show me an entrepreneur with no competition and I will show you an entrepreneur with no market.

Intellectual Property Risk

A lack of awareness and sophistication about IP can be an important risk factor in diligence

Defensive analysis: Are they free to operate without infringing on someone's IP?

Offensive analysis: Can they build IP to protect their space and block competitors?

Can the company develop patents as counter-claims or trading cards in case of an attack on the company?

Legal Risk

What legal issues might be critical for this early stage company?
- Capitalization & Ownership
- Intellectual Property
- Regulatory Compliance
- Third Party Contracts
- Employment Matters

Does the company have its house in order? Is there enough attention being paid to important details?

Alignment Risk

How do you make sure the goals of investors and company founders are in alignment on the following key issues?
- Long term objectives
- Use of funds
- Long term financing path
- Exit assumptions and strategy

Is everyone singing from the same page of the hymnal?

Exit Risk

Exit Strategies
- What are the exit opportunities for the company?
- Who will buy this company?
- When will they buy them?
- What will they value them for?

Equity investment is a loan the ultimate buyer of the company is expected to pay back.

Develop the Investment Thesis

Potential - How big is the potential theoretical opportunity?

Probability - How likely is the company to achieve breakthrough success?

Period - How long are you going to have to wait?

All things being equal, we want companies most likely to be the biggest in the shortest amount of time.

Acknowledge "What Needs to Be Believed"

Core of this exercise is a test… we must ask ourselves:

- Have we identified the key risks?
- Do we understand the premise of the deal (i.e. the investment thesis)?

Are we fooling ourselves, or is there some kind of balanced logic to this deal?

Learning the Hard Way

A handful of avoidable due diligence mistakes

- **Team**: Confusing likability or prior accomplishments with the competence needed to pull off the current task
- **Market**: Confusing early adopter excitement with true market pull
- **Timing**: Is this the right time for this idea?
- **Product**: Incomplete understanding of the dynamics in the target market

Experience is what you get when you don't get what you want.

EVALUATING INVESTMENT OPPORTUNITIES
Appendix

Resources - Due Diligence Checklist

Designed as a quick reference guide to help steer you through the various aspects of diligence. This due diligence checklist covers key items such as:

- Information and documents you need to request from the company
- Tasks your due diligence team needs to perform
- Questions you need to ask of management, customers, references and partners

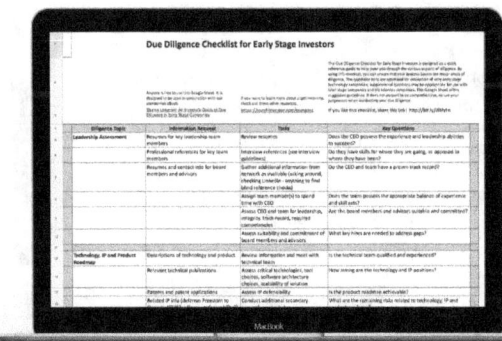

Download Checklist
bit.ly/Due_Diligence_Checklist

Resources - Due Diligence Report Template

The due diligence report template is focused on 11 major topics that should be researched and understood when performing due diligence on an early stage technology company.

For each topic, we provide you with an explanation of the topic as well as example questions that may make sense to discuss in the remarks column.

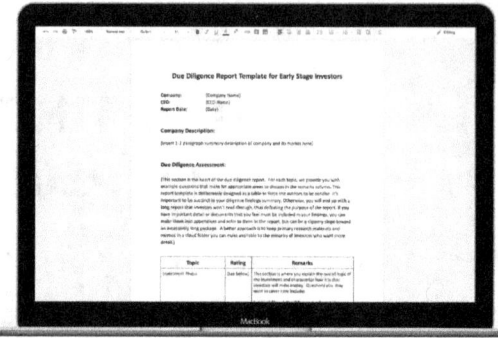

**Download
Report Template**
bit.ly/DueDiligenceReportTemplate

Resources - Management Team Assessment

Questionnaire designed to help guide you through your team reference checks

Focus on questions related to the CEO's:

- Strengths and Weaknesses
- Communications Skills
- Coachability
- Stability
- Domain Expertise
- Complementary Skills on Management Team

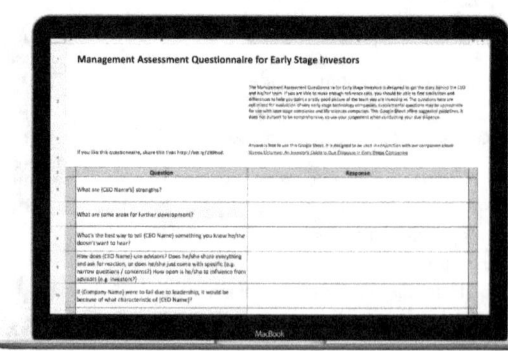

**Download
Questionnaire**
bit.ly/ManagementQuestionnaire

Resources - CEO Performance Review

<u>Questionnaire</u> designed to facilitate the CEO's annual performance review

This best practice is one of the corporate board's most important responsibilities

- Helps build alignment between board members and the CEO
- Improves Board/CEO communications
- Facilitates the future growth and success of the CEO

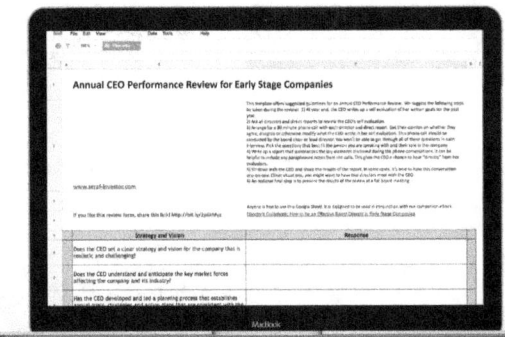

Download
Performance Review
bit.ly/CEOPerformanceReview

Resources - Customer Reference Checks

<u>Questionnaire</u> designed to help guide you through product-related questions

Focus is on questions related to solving a customer's key problems:

- Problem Being Solved and Priority for Solving
- Purchase Reasons and Goals
- Expected ROI and Value to the Customer
- Competitive Factors
- Impressions of the Company and Its Product

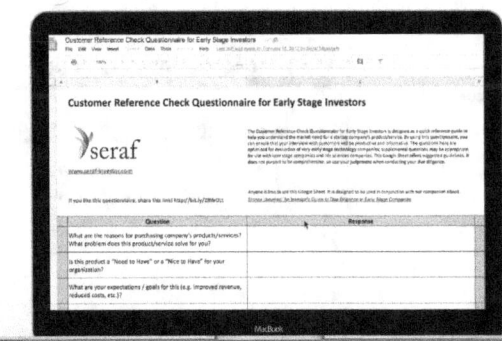

Download
Questionnaire
bit.ly/CustomerReferenceChecks

The Seraf Compass

Continue Your Angel Education and Improve Your Investing Skills

The Seraf Compass guides early stage investors in making better investing decisions, minimizing risk and improving returns

Due Diligence Articles
bit.ly/DueDiligenceArticles

Due Diligence eBook
bit.ly/DueDiligenceEbook

Due Diligence Hardcopy Book
bit.ly/HardCopyBooks

Due Diligence Tools
bit.ly/SerafToolbox

The Seraf Compass

From Investment to Exit: Insights, news, thought leadership and in-depth resources for early stage investors

ACCESS OUR CONTENT
- BLOG
- BOOKS and eBOOKS
- TOOLS

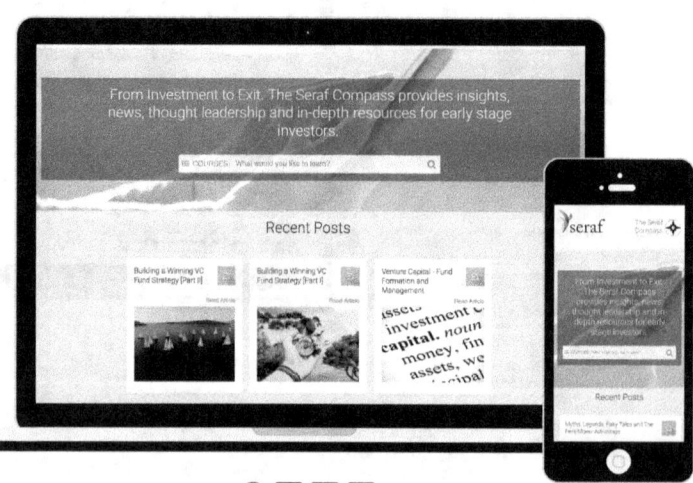

FOLLOW US ON SOCIAL MEDIA

Books from Seraf

Fundamentals of Angel Investing
A Guide to the Principles, Skills and Concepts Every Angel Investor Needs to Succeed

Angel Investing by the Numbers
Valuation, Capitalization, Portfolio Construction and Startup Economics

Leaders Wanted: Making Startup Deals Happen
Advanced Techniques in Deal Leadership and Due Diligence for Early Stage Investors

Guide, Advise and Inspire: How Startup Boards Drive Growth and Exits
An Overview of the Principles, Skills and Concepts Every Early Stage Company Board Member Needs to Succeed

Venture Capital: A Practical Guide
A Guide to Fund Formation and Management

PORTFOLIO MANAGEMENT FOR EARLY STAGE INVESTORS

All Your Info. One Place. Smart Investing.

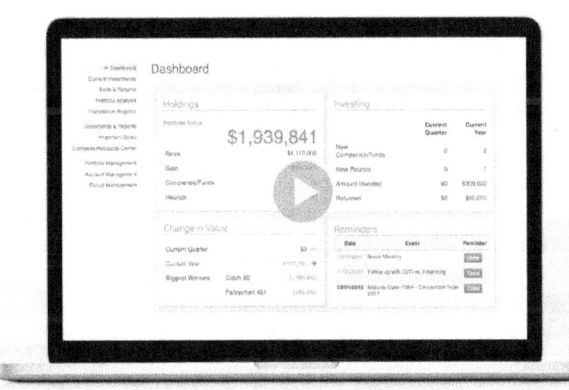

WHAT MAKES SERAF DIFFERENT

Easy Workflow
Seraf guides you through a few easy steps to get your portfolio up and running quickly. Get an overview, develop insights and generate reports in no time.

Deep Experience
Designed by active, early stage investors with over 25 years experience in fund creation and management, the Seraf team understands the complexities of today's early stage investment landscape.

Uniquely Focused Solution
Developed specifically to meet the needs of early stage investors, Seraf provides the tools YOU need to manage your portfolio efficiently.

AUTHORS

Hambleton Lord

Christopher Mirabile

CONTACT US

www.seraf-investor.com

www.angelcapitalassociation.org

EVALUATING INVESTMENT OPPORTUNITIES
Essentials of Due Diligence

Angel Capital Association
World's Largest Association of Active Accredited Investors

ABOUT US

Vision

ACA is recognized as the trusted authority in angel investing.

- 13,000+ Investors
- 250+ Organizations
- Every US State and 5 Canadian Provinces
- Individual Angels, Angel Groups, Accredited Platforms, Family Offices

---

1 EVENTS
Host many international, national and regional events a year

2 EDUCATION
Provide gold standard education for angels

3 PUBLIC POLICY
Leading voice for angels on public policy lobbying in Washington, DC

4 DATA & RESEARCH
Central resource for angel investing data and research

Our Mission

Fuel the success of the accredited investor community through advocacy, education and connection building.

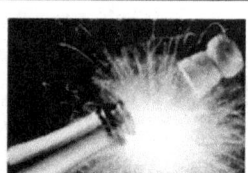

Welcome Message

Seraf's Philosophy

We believe investors in early stage companies should have access to best practices and professional tools to support the entrepreneurial community worldwide and achieve superior outcomes.

Insights and education, combined with powerful portfolio management tools allow investors to understand their investing better, learn faster and make necessary adjustments to select the highest quality opportunities and drive superior returns.

About the Authors

Ham is Co-Founder of Seraf and the Chairman of Launchpad Venture Group, a Boston-based angel group. Through his involvement with Launchpad, Ham has built a personal portfolio of 50+ early stage investments. In addition, he is a board member or board observer with 5 early stage companies.

Christopher is Chair Emeritus of the Angel Capital Association and Managing Director of Launchpad Venture Group. He helps manage Launchpad's portfolio of 70+ companies, he has personally invested in over 65 start-up companies, and is a limited partner in four specialized angel funds. Christopher is a board member, advisor and mentor to numerous start-ups, and a frequent panelist and speaker on entrepreneurship and angel-related topics.

Seraf Co-Founders
Ham Lord & Christopher Mirabile

Presentation Overview

1 **ROLE OF DILIGENCE**
Avoiding Obvious Mistakes

2 **TEAM**
Rule #1: It's All About the Team

3 **PRODUCT**
Product / Technology / Intellectual Property

4 **MARKET**
Market Opportunity / Go-to-Market Strategy / Competition

5 **FINANCIAL**
Financials / Funding / Legal / Exits

6 **CONCLUSION**
WNTBB / Investment Thesis / Lessons Learned

Why Due Diligence is Important

Diligence is not about removing all risk and eliminating all mistakes.

Investing at an early stage - lots of unknowns, there will be failures.

Diligence is about spotting and avoiding the ***obvious*** mistakes.

It's easy to imagine why things might work. It takes effort to grasp subtle and complex ways things can go wrong.

During Due Diligence, You Will...

Spend time with the management team

Educate yourself on the market

Understand the psyche of the target customer

Ask common sense questions

There is no right amount of diligence. Any diligence you do is better than none at all.

3 Guiding Principles of Due Diligence

Identify Key Risks

Develop the Investment Thesis

Acknowledge "What Needs to Be Believed" to Invest

Diligence is not about eliminating all risks and avoiding all mistakes. It's about spotting and avoiding the obvious ones.

Main Areas of Focus in Due Diligence

Team: Are they an "A" team or a "B" team?

Product: Are they selling a "Need to Have" or a "Nice to Have"?

Market: Is the market big enough?

No plan survives contact with the enemy. A great team can assess, learn and adapt quickly to survive and thrive. A good CEO pivots… a great CEO pivots in a capital efficient way.

Why Do We Do It?

A well executed diligence effort increases angel investment returns

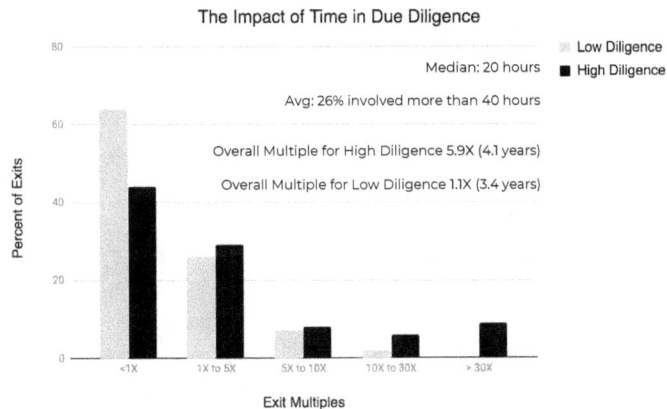

The Impact of Time in Due Diligence

Median: 20 hours
Avg: 26% involved more than 40 hours
Overall Multiple for High Diligence 5.9X (4.1 years)
Overall Multiple for Low Diligence 1.1X (3.4 years)

Mistakes are unavoidable, but racking up easily avoidable mistakes will hurt your overall returns.

EVALUATING INVESTMENT OPPORTUNITIES
Rule #1 - It's All About the Team

Beyond simple reference checks, how do you assess the leadership team?

Required Attributes for Startup Leaders

5 Characteristics typically possessed by a great startup CEO

- Integrity
- Tenacity
- IQ/EQ
- Deep Market Understanding
- Presence

This is a demanding job calling for an unusual set of traits and temperament

---

Evaluating the CEO

Reference Checks

- Provided by CEO, in addition to other blind references from your network
- Identify red flags and indicate areas to apply resources in future to help make CEO successful

It takes a long time to get to know people. Supercharge your review by talking to people who've known the CEO for a long time.

Evaluating the CEO

Spend time one-on-one with CEO in an appropriate non-business setting
- Get to know CEO in a different context
- Begin building a long term professional relationship

Anyone can fool you for a little while, nobody can fool you forever - time is everything.

The Role of Domain-Specific Experience

Important: When building a next generation product in a well established market

Not Important: When looking to create a new market or totally disrupt an existing market

Even if it is a speculative new market, expect your CEO to deeply understand the customer and the customer problem.

Key Skills for a Complete Founding Team

A high functioning team is more than a group of high functioning individuals

Look for following skills represented in one or more of team members

- Ability to Sell
- Technical Knowledge
- Deep Market Awareness
- Product Management Skills

Project your thinking into the future. Just because they are smart and accomplished doesn't mean what they know is useful or even relevant to where they are going.

Size of a Founding Team

2 to 3 Founders with Complementary Skills

    Don't invest in a one-person team

More than 4 founders can result in the following issues

    Coattail riders, founder dilution…

Adding founders is disruptive, as is outgrowing and shedding founders.

EVALUATING INVESTMENT OPPORTUNITIES

Product / Technology / Intellectual Property

Can you find enough people who are hungry to buy your product at a price that leaves you with a good profit?

How to Determine if a Product is Oxygen or Aspirin

Reach out to current customers and prospects and ask:

- What problem does the product solve for you?
- On your list of top problems in your organization, where does solving this problem fall on your priority list?

The answers to these two questions will go a long way in determining whether the product "Is a 'Nice-to-Have' or a 'Need-to-Have'?

What must you understand to determine if a company has breakthrough technology?

Is the Product Differentiated?

Ask customers and prospects the following:

- How are you solving your problem today?
- Have you used similar products before?
- Did you look at any competitive products?
- Are you considering any alternative ways of solving the problem?

Your job is to figure out differentiators that actually matter to the customer and make sure they are in the product.

What's Needed for a High Level Technology Assessment?

Assuming the product works and is in the hands of customers, you should ask the following:

- Is the new product significantly better/faster/cheaper than the incumbents?
- Will the benefits described by the CEO and verified by customers result in significant value for the customer?

The inertia of "good enough" is an enormous force to overcome - if it isn't 10X better, faster or cheaper, it may cost too much to sell.

What About a Product Roadmap?

Markets evolve constantly. Successful companies need strong product management to navigate in this environment.

- Is there a product roadmap?
- Who wrote and owns it?
- What's on it, what was left off, and why?
- How far does it go into the future?
- What are some specific examples of things that the team said "no" to upon arriving at this roadmap?

A company that can really hold their own in a detailed product roadmap review has a lot less technical risk than one that can't.

How do you evaluate the importance and strength of the company's Intellectual Property?

Is the Product Defensible?

Does the company have a compelling offering that will allow them to keep their customers and maintain their pricing power?

Can they keep competition out with some form of IP (e.g. patents, trade secrets)?

Can they keep customers hooked through high switching costs?

They are going to have to find a way to either keep competitors locked out or keep customers locked in.

What About the Technology Team?

If a company is tech-centric, tech skills need to be part of the founding team

Tech can be outsourced when it's an enabler of company's solution, but not when it's core to company. Beware the following:

- Outsourced tech tends to move slower than in-house tech
- Cost savings are rarely achieved due to communication and coordination issues
- Potential acquirers often place a lower valuation on a company using outsourced tech

A tech company with no tech team is going to get worse gas mileage with your money and fall behind the competition over time.

What About the Technology Team?

If a company is tech-centric, tech skills need to be part of the founding team

Tech can be outsourced when it's an enabler of company's solution, but not when it's core to company. Beware the following:

- Outsourced tech tends to move slower than in-house tech
- Cost savings are rarely achieved due to communication and coordination issues
- Potential acquirers often place a lower valuation on a company using outsourced tech

A tech company with no tech team is going to get worse gas mileage with your money and fall behind the competition over time.

EVALUATING INVESTMENT OPPORTUNITIES

Market Opportunity / Go-to-Market Strategy / Competition

Is there enough of a market to build a big business when using reasonable market share projections?

Characteristics of an Investable Market Opportunity

A market worth going after offers an opportunity to build a steep growth curve

- **Established Markets**: Look for companies that can disrupt the market to grow faster than the overall market and take market share from the leaders
- **New Markets**: Look for companies that can educate and acquire customers for a cost less than the lifetime value of those customers

Startups are like hang-gliders. They are looking for market "thermals" that allow them to gain altitude despite gravity pulling them down.

What's the Minimum Size in a Potential Market?

Early stage investors are looking for 10X returns

For a $100M market size, really aggressive assumptions are required:

- Angels own 25% of the company after $4M in investment
- Company achieves 40% market share
- Company acquired for 4X multiple of revenue

It's hard to make the math work on less than a $100M Market

Accurately Sizing a Market Opportunity

Assess customer buying priorities

How much are the customers willing to pay?

Market size is really a question of sales and marketing spend - at your price, how many customers can you get for a price that is more than you spend acquiring them?

Timing is Everything

Is this the **right time** for this idea?
- Are you going to catch a big wave or a little wave?
- Where is the wave... far away, nearby or just past?

If you start paddling too early, you will run out of steam before the wave arrives. If you start paddling too late, the wave will pass under you and not propel you forward.

Applying the 3 "P"s to Selecting Investments

Potential - How big is the potential theoretical opportunity?

Probability - How likely is the company to achieve breakthrough success?

Period - How long are you going to have to wait?

All things being equal, we want companies most likely to be the biggest in the shortest amount of time.

Does the company have the right initial strategy for selling to the customer and a plan for doing it at scale?

Evaluating Go-to-Market Strategies

How is the company selling the product?
- Direct sales force
- Over the web
- Through partners or distributors

Choice of distribution channel is a significant factor in sales and marketing costs.

Evaluating Go-to-Market Strategies

Where are the customers and how will they locate them, talk to them, and bring them on board cost-effectively?

What is the customer acquisition cost (CAC) going to be relative to the lifetime value (LTV) of the customer?

You can't spend $1000 acquiring a $500 customer. Ideally, LTV to CAC will be at least 3:1 or 4:1 to achieve profitability.

Evaluating Go-to-Market Strategies

For startups, **focus and prioritization** are everything

Resources should be **spent wisely** and in a targeted way

Companies **over extend** limited resources by going after any opportunity

More companies die from overeating than starvation.

Evaluating Early Stage Sales Teams

What does a **startup sales team** look like?

- Expect a small team where the CEO might be the chief salesperson
- A VP Sales should have a startup company background and the ability to carry a sales quota in the early days

Early stage sales is all about figuring out what produces results before you spend big bucks scaling the sales organization

Evaluating Early Stage Marketing Teams

Where are the marketing team's resources focused?

- **Market Segmentation**: Who is the target customer(s)?
- **Market Opportunity**: How many customers are out there? How much are they willing to spend?
- **Marketing Channels**: Where will you find them? How will you reach them?

Early marketing programs should involve lots of experimentation and testing before the spend is scaled up.

Product / Market Fit

Does the company have a product that meets the needs of a large market?

Are leads growing, sales cycles shortening, and revenue per customer climbing?

Limited data in early stage companies makes it tough to determine product / market fit. Anyone can sell to the small percentage of the market that consists of early adopters.

What is the competitive environment including but not limited to the set of competitors that the company identifies? What will the competition be in 5 years?

Four Fierce Competitors for All Startups

Ignorance about the product

Alternates/substitutes from other categories

Fear of change

The inertia of "good enough"

Show me an entrepreneur "with no competition" and I will show you a company with no market!

Is the Product Differentiated?

Look for distinctions that matter to the customer

- How are you solving your problem today?
- Have you used similar products before?
- Did you look at any competitive products?
- Are you considering any alternative ways of solving the problem?

Founders love features; customers care about benefits.

Is the Product Defensible?

Retaining customers and protecting margins requires a strong value proposition

- Can the hard won customers be retained?
- Will pricing power hold up over time?
- Are the margins in the business likely to be squeezed by competitive or environmental factors?

No point in fighting to take a hill if you can't stay on top of it long enough to take in the view.

How Does Competition Affect Market Opportunity?

Not necessarily the way you might think…

Here are 4 ways that competition can be helpful:

- Helps **bear cost** and workload of **educating the market**
- Legitimizes and **reduces perceived risk** of new product category
- Attracts **enabling services** and technologies
- Attracts analysts and an **ecosystem** around product

It's not whether your product has competitors, it's whether your product is competitive.

EVALUATING INVESTMENT OPPORTUNITIES
Financials / Funding / Legal / Exits

After digging into the financial model do you feel the key assumptions are reasonable and the near term milestones are achievable with this current round of financing?

Financial Plan: Key Assumptions and Milestones

A well thought out financial plan needs two elements:

FIRST:

Key assumptions that are both **rational** and **verifiable**

If the assumptions don't pass the sniff test, the financial plan won't hold together.

Financial Plan: Key Assumptions and Milestones

A well thought out financial plan needs two elements:

SECOND:

Achievable milestones which **significantly increase** the company's **value**

Will new investors be interested in continuing to finance the company at a higher valuation after this round of funding is spent?

What is the long term funding strategy of the company and how will different strategies impact the early investors?

Long Term Funding Plan

A well-thought-out funding plan needs:

- A clear understanding of **how much runway** the company has before it runs out of cash
- The **long term capital requirements** before the company has an exit

Do you understand how much future financing risk you are taking by making this investment?

What legal issues are critical with an early stage company in areas such as regulation, contracts, IP and employment?

Legal Issues

Early stage investors undertake legal diligence in these 4 areas:
- Intellectual Property
- Corporate Capitalization Structure
- Third Party Contracts
- Employment Agreements

Don't take shortcuts here… get help if necessary and put in the time so you don't miss an issue that could severely impact the company's long term value.

What are the exit opportunities for the company? Who buys this company? Why do they value it and what might they pay?

Exit Opportunities

A great startup CEO should be able to answer 5 questions:

QUESTION ONE

What makes this company interesting to potential buyers?

Why is anyone going to care about this company?

Exit Opportunities

A great startup CEO should be able to answer 5 questions:

QUESTION TWO

Who are the potential buyers?

Who is going to care about this company?

Exit Opportunities

A great startup CEO should be able to answer 5 questions:

QUESTION THREE

What milestones are going to need to be achieved before the company is a candidate for acquisition?

How far do investors have to fund this?

Exit Opportunities

A great startup CEO should be able to answer 5 questions:

QUESTION FOUR

What is the likely price range to be paid for an acquisition?

One good comparable deal is a fluke, two is interesting, three is a trend.

Exit Opportunities

A great startup CEO should be able to answer 5 questions:

QUESTION FIVE

Is this company a credible candidate for an IPO?

These days angels can expect to get an IPO about as often as a golfer can expect to get a hole in one.

How do the deal terms, funding strategy and exit opportunities combine to produce a reward that justifies the risk of an early stage investment?

Deal Terms and Payoff

Valuation is not the only factor that matters.

Deal terms can greatly affect your outcome upon exit.

All key deal terms can be categorized into four buckets:

- Economics
- Investor Rights & Protection
- Governance, Management & Control
- Exits & Liquidity

Old VC joke: "You pick the valuation, and I'll pick the deal terms."

Deal Terms and Payoff

Deal Economics:
- Valuation
- Size of Round
- Preferences
- Option Pool
- Dividends

Deal Terms and Payoff

Investor Rights & Protections:
- Anti-dilution
- Approval rights
- Participation Rights
- ROFR & Co-Sale Rights

Deal Terms and Payoff

Governance, Management & Control:

- Board Seats
- Information rights
- Founder Vesting
- Protective Provisions

Deal Terms and Payoff

Exits & Liquidity:

- Rights to block transfers
- Drag-along rights
- Redemption rights
- Registration rights

How do you make sure that the goals of the investors and the company founders are in alignment?

Verifying Goal Alignment

Investors and Management should verify alignment with:

- Long term company objectives
- Use of funds and aggressiveness of investment levels
- Long range financing plan and assumptions
- Exit strategies and expectations on size and timing

I don't know where I am going, but I'm making good time!

EVALUATING INVESTMENT OPPORTUNITIES
Conclusion

Develop the Investment Thesis

Potential - How big is the potential theoretical opportunity?

Probability - How likely is the company to achieve breakthrough success?

Period - How long are you going to have to wait?

All things being equal, we want companies most likely to be the biggest in the shortest amount of time.

Acknowledge "What Needs to Be Believed"

Core of this exercise is a test… we must ask ourselves:
- Have we identified the key risks?
- Do we understand the premise of the deal (i.e. the investment thesis)?

Are we fooling ourselves, or is there some kind of balanced logic to this deal?

Learning the Hard Way

A handful of avoidable due diligence mistakes
- **Team**: Confusing likability or prior accomplishments with the competence needed to pull off the current task
- **Market**: Confusing early adopter excitement with true market pull
- **Timing**: Is this the right time for this idea?
- **Product**: Incomplete understanding of the dynamics in the target market

Experience is what you get when you don't get what you want.

EVALUATING INVESTMENT OPPORTUNITIES
Appendix

Resources - Due Diligence Checklist

Designed as a quick reference guide to help steer you through the various aspects of diligence. This due diligence checklist covers key items such as:

- Information and documents you need to request from the company
- Tasks your due diligence team needs to perform
- Questions you need to ask of management, customers, references and partners

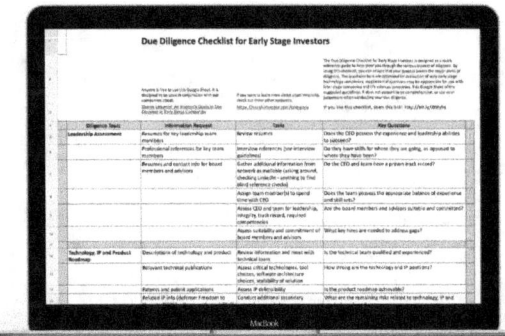

Download Checklist
bit.ly/Due_Diligence_Checklist

Resources - Due Diligence Report Template

The due diligence report template is focused on 11 major topics that should be researched and understood when performing due diligence on an early stage technology company.

For each topic, we provide you with an explanation of the topic as well as example questions that may make sense to discuss in the remarks column.

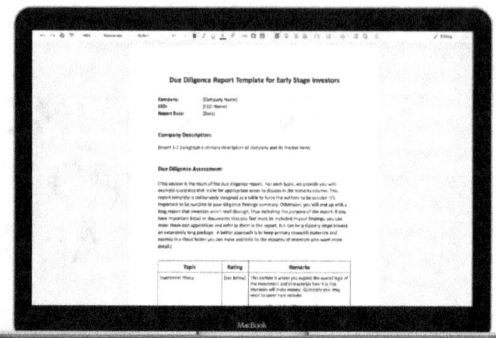

**Download
Report Template**
bit.ly/DueDiligenceReportTemplate

Resources - Management Team Assessment

Questionnaire designed to help guide you through your team reference checks

Focus on questions related to the CEO's:

- Strengths and Weaknesses
- Communications Skills
- Coachability
- Stability
- Domain Expertise
- Complementary Skills on Management Team

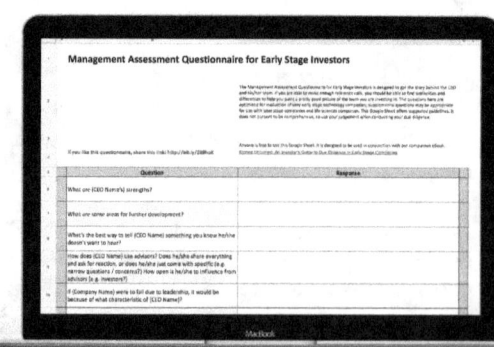

**Download
Questionnaire**
bit.ly/ManagementQuestionnaire

Resources - CEO Performance Review

<u>Questionnaire</u> designed to facilitate the CEO's annual performance review

This best practice is one of the corporate board's most important responsibilities

- Helps build alignment between board members and the CEO
- Improves Board/CEO communications
- Facilitates the future growth and success of the CEO

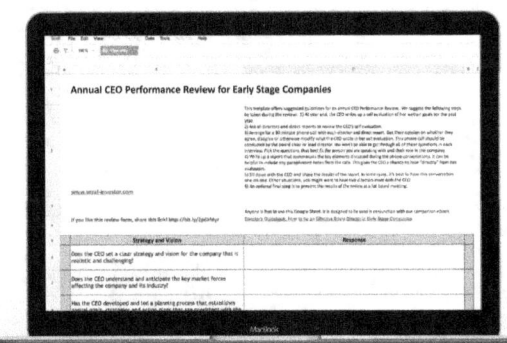

Download
Performance Review
bit.ly/CEOPerformanceReview

Resources - Customer Reference Checks

<u>Questionnaire</u> designed to help guide you through product-related questions

Focus is on questions related to solving a customer's key problems:

- Problem Being Solved and Priority for Solving
- Purchase Reasons and Goals
- Expected ROI and Value to the Customer
- Competitive Factors
- Impressions of the Company and Its Product

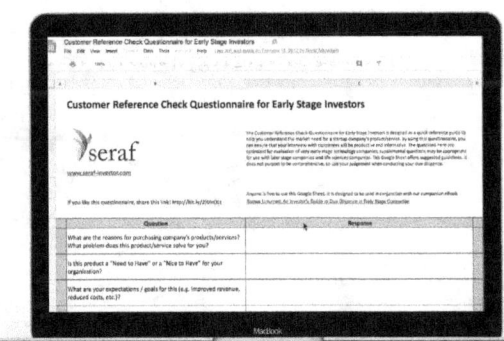

Download
Questionnaire
bit.ly/CustomerReferenceChecks

Continue Your Angel Education
and Improve Your Investing Skills

The Seraf Compass guides early stage investors in making better investing decisions, minimizing risk and improving returns

Due Diligence Articles
bit.ly/DueDiligenceArticles

Due Diligence eBook
bit.ly/DueDiligenceEbook

Due Diligence Hardcopy Book
bit.ly/HardCopyBooks

Due Diligence Tools
bit.ly/SerafToolbox

From Investment to Exit: Insights, news, thought leadership and in-depth resources for early stage investors

ACCESS OUR CONTENT

BLOG

BOOKS and eBOOKS

TOOLS

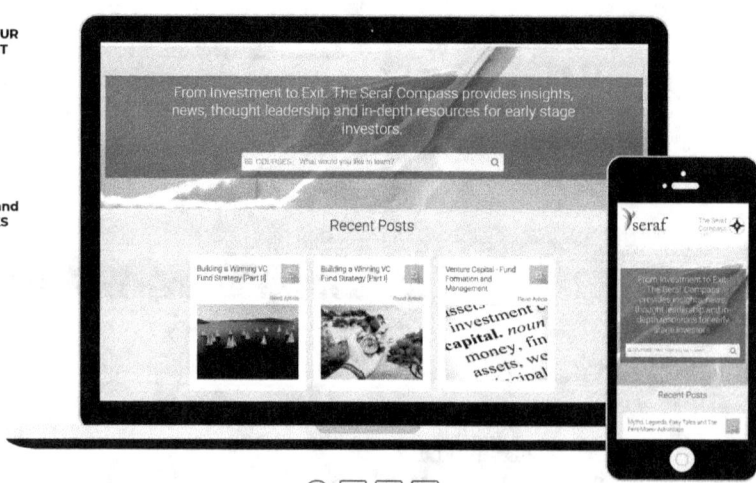

FOLLOW US ON SOCIAL MEDIA

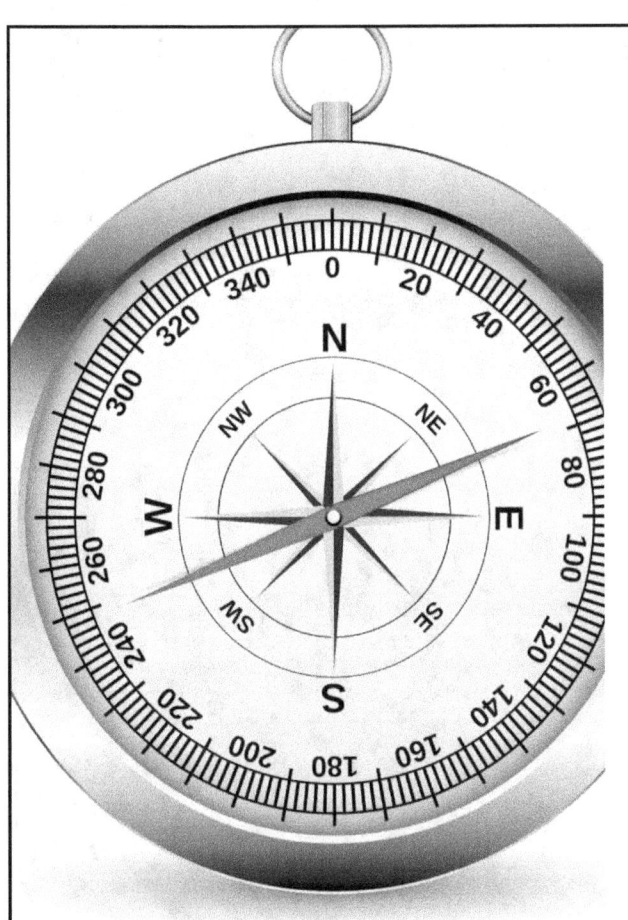

Books from Seraf

Fundamentals of Angel Investing
A Guide to the Principles, Skills and Concepts Every Angel Investor Needs to Succeed

Angel Investing by the Numbers
Valuation, Capitalization, Portfolio Construction and Startup Economics

Leaders Wanted: Making Startup Deals Happen
Advanced Techniques in Deal Leadership and Due Diligence for Early Stage Investors

Guide, Advise and Inspire: How Startup Boards Drive Growth and Exits
An Overview of the Principles, Skills and Concepts Every Early Stage Company Board Member Needs to Succeed

Venture Capital: A Practical Guide
A Guide to Fund Formation and Management

PORTFOLIO MANAGEMENT FOR EARLY STAGE INVESTORS
All Your Info. One Place. Smart Investing.

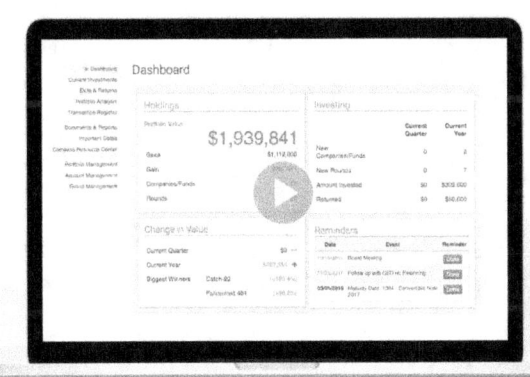

WHAT MAKES SERAF DIFFERENT

Easy Workflow
Seraf guides you through a few easy steps to get your portfolio up and running quickly. Get an overview, develop insights and generate reports in no time.

Deep Experience
Designed by active, early stage investors with over 25 years experience in fund creation and management, the Seraf team understands the complexities of today's early stage investment landscape.

Uniquely Focused Solution
Developed specifically to meet the needs of early stage investors, Seraf provides the tools YOU need to manage your portfolio efficiently.

AUTHORS

Hambleton Lord

Christopher Mirabile

CONTACT US

www.seraf-investor.com

www.angelcapitalassociation.org

Appendix

In this appendix, we provide a series of templates to help facilitate the due diligence process.

Due Diligence Report: This template is designed to result in a short, readable due diligence report. Our goal at Launchpad is to provide our investors with a 2 to 4 page summary report that is readable and comprehensive. It covers all the main areas in diligence and provides the author(s) with a structured approach. (htttps://bit.ly/DueDiligenceReportTemplate)

Due Diligence Checklist: After reading this book, you might feel overwhelmed by all the different aspects in due diligence. The Due Diligence Checklist is designed as a quick reference guide to help steer you through the various aspects of diligence. (https://bit.ly/Due_Diligence_Checklist)

Customer Reference Check Questionnaire: At the core of this questionnaire are a series of questions that will help you distinguish whether the company is selling aspirin, oxygen or jewelry. And, you can find out a bit more about the size of the potential market opportunity. (https://bit.ly/CustomerReferenceChecks)

Management Assessment Questionnaire: This questionnaire is designed to get the story behind the CEO and his/her team. If you are able to make enough reference calls, you should be able to find similarities and differences to help you paint a pretty good picture of the team you are investing in. (https://bit.ly/ManagementQuestionnaire)

Versions of each of these documents are available online. If you go to the URL next to each item, you will be able to access an online document that will save you time in creating your own copy of these documents.

Due Diligence Report

This template is designed to result in a short, readable due diligence report. Our goal is to provide our investors with a 2 to 4 page summary report that is readable and comprehensive. It covers all the main areas in diligence and provides the author(s) with a structured approach.

Company: {Company Name}

CEO: {CEO Name}

Report Date: {Date}

Company Description:

{insert 1-2 paragraph summary description of company here}

Due Diligence Assessment:

{This section is the heart of the due diligence report. For each topic, we provide you with example questions that make for appropriate areas to discuss in the remarks column. This report template is deliberately designed as a table to force the authors to be concise. It's important to be succinct in your diligence findings summary. Otherwise, you will end up with a long report that investors won't read through, thus defeating the purpose of the report. If you have important detail or documents that you feel must be included in your findings, you can make them into appendices and refer to them in the report, but can be a slippery slope toward an excessively long package. A better approach is to keep primary research materials and memos in a cloud folder you can make available to the minority of investors who want more detail.}

Topic	Rating	Remarks
Investment Thesis		
What Needs To Be Believed (WNTBB)		
Failure Risk		
Leadership Assessment		
Technology, IP and Product Roadmap		
Customer Need and Go-To-Market Plan		
Uniqueness and Competition		
Market Size and Market Opportunity		
Financial Projections and Funding Strategy		
Exit Strategy		
Deal Terms and Payoff		

Individual Assessments:

{This section of the report is designed to allow each member of the due diligence team to provide some short feedback on their personal opinion of the investment opportunity. You shouldn't expect everyone's assessment to be positive. In fact, it's important to have at least one or two dissenting opinions to add balance to the report. And, make sure to ask for succinct summary comments. It is especially helpful if each commenter ends their comments with a note about whether they plan to invest and why/why not.}

Team Member	Rating	Summary Remarks
{Name 1}		
{Name 2}		
{Name 3}		

Key

(++) = Very Positive (+) = Positive (0) = Neutral

(–) = Negative but issues can be overcome

(/)Very Negative, issues cannot be overcome

Investment Thesis: This section is where you explain the overall logic of the investment and characterize how it is that investors will make money. Questions you may want to cover here include:

- Is this a billion dollar IPO opportunity or is it more likely to be acquired for under $50M? Or something in between?
- Are there limited number of risks that can be mitigated or is this a moonshot deal with big risk and potentially big reward?
- Will it take 10 years to complete the product and get FDA approval, or could this company be acquired in the first couple of years by a big competitor?

What Needs to Be Believed (WNTBB): This section is where you boil down all of the key risks that need to be assumed in order to invest (see companion eBook for more detail). If an investor cannot make peace with or cannot believe an item on this list can be overcome, she should not invest. Example WNTBBs might include:

- That this market can be disrupted.
- That enough customers will find this essential at this price point.
- That the company will be successful in transitioning from current niche to mainstream.
- That the company can build out a successful go to market plan and demonstrate traction on this round size.
- That this management team can scale to pull this off.
- That the company can achieve market share before the large competitors crowd them out.

Failure Risk: This section is where you talk about the main weaknesses in the plan and the degree to which they are mitigated. If this company fails is it likely for lack of capitalization, inability to make the technology work, competition?

Leadership Assessment: This section is where you discuss your assessment of the management team. Questions you may want to cover here include:

- Does the CEO possess the experience and leadership abilities to succeed?
- Do they have skills for where they are going, as opposed to where they have been?
- Do the CEO and team have a proven track record?

- Does the team possess the appropriate balance of experience and skill sets?
- Are the board members and advisors suitable and committed?
- What key hires are needed to address gaps?

Technology, IP and Product Roadmap: This section is where you discuss your assessment of the technology and technology risk as well as the IP situation. Questions you may want to cover here include:

- Is the technical team qualified and experienced?
- How strong are the technology and IP positions?
- Is there a product roadmap and is it achievable?
- What are the remaining risks related to technology, IP and product roadmap?
- Are their superior technologies on the near term horizon?

Customer Need and Go-To-Market Plan: This section is where you discuss your assessment of the plan to take the product to market. Questions you may want to cover here include:

- Is the GTM plan sufficiently detailed?
- Are the assumptions, including required level of sales spend and time lines reasonable?
- Is the sales pipeline adequate, and are key metrics for adoption rate, conversion rates, etc. conservative?
- Do customers confirm the need and likely adoption rates?
- Beyond verifying some demand, do we understand the customers buying priorities? Is this Oxygen, Aspirin or Jewelry?
- What are the major risks in marketing awareness, customer adoption rates and sales cycle?

Uniqueness and Competition: This section is where you discuss your assessment of the overall competitiveness and defensibility of the offering. Questions you may want to cover here include:

- Is the company well positioned with respect to current and likely future competitors?
- Is the founding team well-informed about their market and industry? Do they have a good competitive sense, or are they unaware of key issues?

- What are the major risks in marketing awareness, customer adoption rates and sales cycle?

Market Size and Market Opportunity: This section is where you discuss your assessment of the actual addressable market. Questions you may want to cover here include:

- Are the top-down and bottoms-up market estimates consistent and attractive?
- Are the market share projections reasonable?
- What are the remaining risks in market development?

Financial Projections and Funding Strategy: This section is where you discuss your assessment of the financial plan and capital raising strategy. Questions you may want to cover here include:

- Does the balance sheet make sense, and are there any showstopper issues?
- Are the financial projections reasonable and conservative in light of past performance?
- What are the implications of variances in key assumptions?
- Is the future financing risk manageable?
- What are remaining financial risks?
- Are the assumptions about scaling expense (e.g. G&A, etc.) reasonable, or is the model unrealistic?

Exit Strategy: This section is where you discuss your assessment of the likely exit opportunities. Questions you may want to cover here include:

- Is there alignment with the CEO and team on exit goals?
- Is the exit strategy reasonable?
- Is the assumed timeline reasonable?
- What exit multiples can be predicted under representative scenarios?
- Does the CEO know people in the industry? Is he/she a networker who will make the relationships and do the thought-leadership necessary to get a buyer interested?

Deal Terms and Payoff: This section is where you summarize the relationship between the deal terms in the termsheet and the expected investor return. Questions you may want to cover here include:

- Is this a low valuation, high risk deal, or a high valuation, low risk deal?
- Does the termsheet include specific terms intended to protect this round of investors?
- Can you show the desired return multiple based on exit multiples for comparable companies?

Due Diligence Checklist

This checklist is designed to be appropriate for early stage investments. The "Information Request" and "Tasks" columns list those items and tasks, respectively, that are generally required, at a minimum, to complete diligence. The "Key Questions" column is representative of typical questions the diligence effort should address. The information request, tasks, and key questions should all be reviewed and revised, as needed, for the particular situation. The "Summary Points" column may be used by the team to summarize the answers to key questions in preparation for drafting the diligence report. Thank you to Launchpad member Gail Greenwald for her help developing this checklist.

Leadership Assessment

Information Request	Tasks	Key Questions
Resumes for key leadership team members	Review resumes	Does the CEO possess the experience and leadership abilities to succeed?
Professional references for key team members	Interview references (see interview guidelines)	Do they have skills for where they are going, as opposed to where they have been?
Resumes and contact info for board members and advisors	Gather additional information from network as available (asking around, checking LinkedIn - anything to find blind reference checks)	Do the CEO and team have a proven track record?
	Assign team member(s) to spend time with CEO	Does the team possess the appropriate balance of experience and skill sets?
	Assess CEO and team for leadership, integrity, track record, required competencies	Are the board members and advisors suitable and committed?
	Assess suitability and commitment of board members and advisors	What key hires are needed to address gaps?

Technology, IP and Product Roadmap

Information Request	Tasks	Key Questions
Descriptions of technology and product	Review information and meet with technical team	Is the technical team qualified and experienced?
Relevant technical publications	Assess critical technologies, tool choices, software architecture choices, scalability of solution	How strong are the technology and IP positions?
Patents and patent applications	Assess IP defensibility	Is the product roadmap achievable?
Related IP info (defense: Freedom to Operate (FTO)?, offense: enforceability?)	Conduct additional secondary research as needed	What are the remaining risks related to technology, IP and product roadmap?
Product roadmap with key milestones	Conduct additional expert interviews if needed	Are their superior technologies on the near term horizon?
Competing technologies and commercialization status	Assess remaining technical risk, IP defensibility, competitive technical position	

Regulatory Strategy

Information Request	Tasks	Key Questions
Regulatory strategy, if relevant	Review regulatory strategy	Is the regulatory strategy well thought through and feasible?
Status of dialogue with regulatory authorities and/or consultants, copies of relevant communications	Interview regulatory experts	Are the company's financial resources sufficient to implement the regulatory plan?
	Assess comparable regulatory pathways for other products as appropriate	Are assumptions about partners/acquirers' roles in the regulatory plan reasonable?
	Assess regulatory climate	What are the remaining regulatory risks?

Customer Need and Go-to-Market Plan

Information Request	Tasks	Key Questions
Go-to-market plan with key milestones and granular detail on sales approach	Review information and meet with marketing and sales team	Is the GTM plan reasonable?
Partner identification and relationship status	Interview customers, partners, prospects as appropriate	Is the sales pipeline adequate, and are key metrics for adoption rate, conversion rates, etc. conservative?
Sales pipeline by stage, factored to be truly realistic and achievable	Gather information on industry comparisons as appropriate	Do customers confirm the need and likely adoption rates?
Any current marketing, joint venture, distribution agreements	Collaborate with financial team to assess revenue and pricing model	Beyond verifying some demand, do we understand the customers buying priorities? Is this Oxygen, Aspirin or Jewelry?
Customer, prospect, and partner references (see guidelines for interviewing customers)		What are the major risks in marketing awareness, customer adoption rates and sales cycle?

Uniqueness and Competition

Information Request	Tasks	Key Questions
List of current and prospective competitors	Gather additional competitive intelligence as needed	Is the company well positioned with respect to current and likely future competitors?
Competitive analysis including market share, relative strengths and weaknesses	Assess competitive environment, competitor positions, barriers to entry	Is the founding team well-informed about their market and industry? Do they have a good competitive sense, or are they unaware of key issues?
		What are the major risks in marketing awareness, customer adoption rates and sales cycle?

Customer Reference Check Questionnaire

At the core of this questionnaire are a series of questions that will help you distinguish whether the company is selling aspirin, oxygen or jewelry. And, you can find out a bit more about the size of the potential market opportunity.

Customer Reference Check Questionnaire

What are the reasons for purchasing company's products/services? What problem does this product/service solve for you?
Is this product a "Need to Have" or a "Nice to Have" for your organization?
What are your expectations / goals for this (e.g. improved revenue, reduced costs, etc.)?
Does the ROI for this product justify the current pricing? Would you expect to pay more or less for the product?
Have you used similar products/services before?
On your list of the top problems in your organization, where does solving this problem fall on your priority list?
Is your company generally an early or late adopter of new solutions?
Which products/services from the company do you use? Do you expect to add additional products/services in the future?
Did you look at any competitive products?
Why did you select company over other competitors?
As a customer/prospect for (company's) products/services, how did your interaction with the company go? Did they meet your expectations?
What is your impression of the company's management team?

Management Assessment Questionnaire

This questionnaire is designed to get the story behind the CEO and his/her team. If you are able to make enough reference calls, you should be able to find similarities and differences to help you paint a pretty good picture of the team you are investing in.

Management Assessment Questionnaire

What are {CEO Name's} strengths?

What are some areas for further development?

What's the best way to tell {CEO Name} something you know he/she doesn't want to hear?

How does {CEO Name} use advisors? Does he/she share everything and ask for reaction, or does he/she just come with specific (e.g. narrow questions / concerns?) How open is he/she to influence from advisors (e.g. investors?)

If {Company Name} were to fail due to leadership, it would be because of what characteristic of {CEO Name}?

Does {CEO Name} show sufficient emotional intelligence to be able to navigate the typical ups and downs of an early stage company?

Do one or more members of the management team have a proven track record and does prior track record include successful exit(s)/returned money to investors?

Does the management team have applicable domain expertise?

Does the management team have complementary skills?

www.ingramcontent.com/pod-product-compliance
Lightning Source LLC
Chambersburg PA
CBHW062356220526
45472CB00008B/1829